Piazzas

Many older Charleston homes were built with beautiful piazzas and verandas that were enjoyed by all throughout the year. The heat and humidity of Charleston made it necessary to open windows and doors so breezes could flow through the house. Covered areas like piazzas and verandas allowed doors and windows to remain open while protecting the home's interior from blowing rain and beating sun. Open windows located on the opposite wall promoted cross ventilation.

The Historic
Charleston Foundation

Nathaniel Russell House

(c. 1808)

Owned by the Historic Charleston Foundation, the
Nathaniel Russell House was built in 1808 for one of
Charleston's most prominent merchants. The Russell
House is one of America's most important neo-classical
residences and is open to the public.

Edmondston-Alston House

The Edmondston-Alston House has a panoramic view of the Charleston harbor. Built c. 1825, the house is a splendid example of the Greek Revival style. Open to the public.

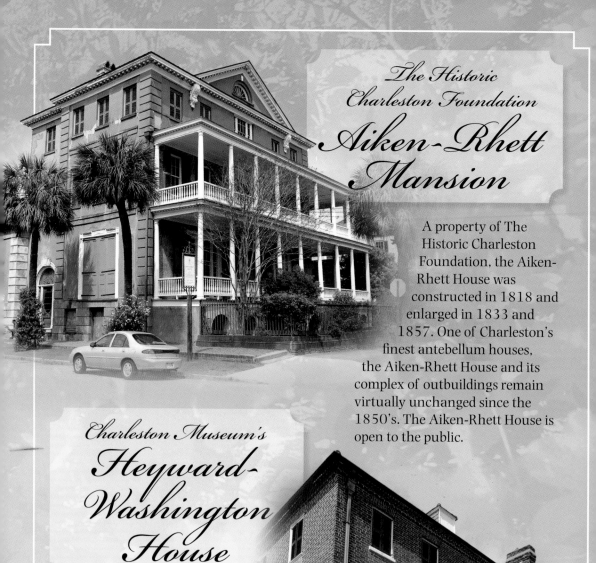

The Historic Charleston Foundation
Aiken-Rhett Mansion

A property of The Historic Charleston Foundation, the Aiken-Rhett House was constructed in 1818 and enlarged in 1833 and 1857. One of Charleston's finest antebellum houses, the Aiken-Rhett House and its complex of outbuildings remain virtually unchanged since the 1850's. The Aiken-Rhett House is open to the public.

Charleston Museum's
Heyward-Washington House

The Heyward-Washington House (c. 1772), is a three-story "double house." Thomas Heyward, Jr., signer of the Declaration of Independence, lived in this house. George Washington lodged here when the President visited Charleston in 1791. Magnificent Charleston-made furniture enhances this beautiful house. A formal 18th century garden is in the rear. Owned and operated by The Charleston Museum. Open year round. Admission.

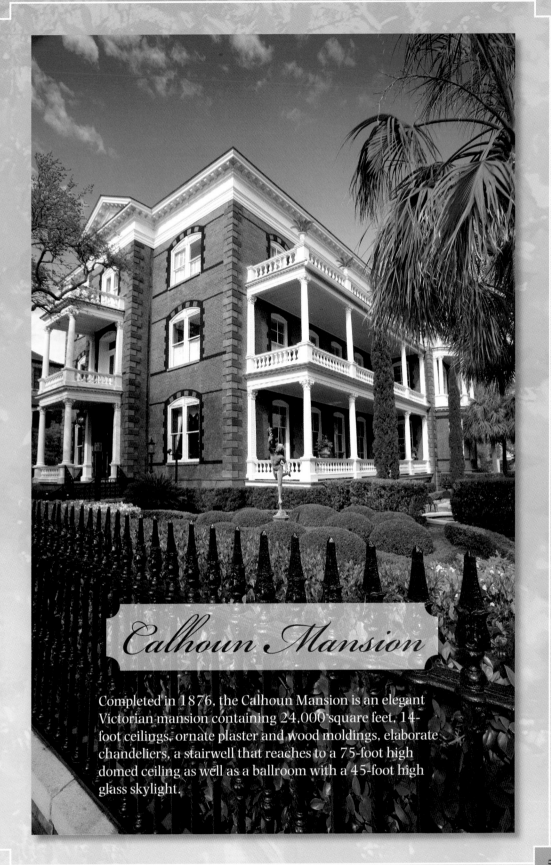

Calhoun Mansion

Completed in 1876, the Calhoun Mansion is an elegant Victorian mansion containing 24,000 square feet, 14-foot ceilings, ornate plaster and wood moldings, elaborate chandeliers, a stairwell that reaches to a 75-foot high domed ceiling as well as a ballroom with a 45-foot high glass skylight.

Charleston Museum's

Joseph Manigault House

The Joseph Manigault House (c. 1803), is one of the outstanding examples of Adam architecture in America. This elegance makes it one of the most distinguished houses in the city. The house was designed by Gabriel Manigault for his brother Joseph. Owned and administered by the Charleston Museum. Open year round. Admission.

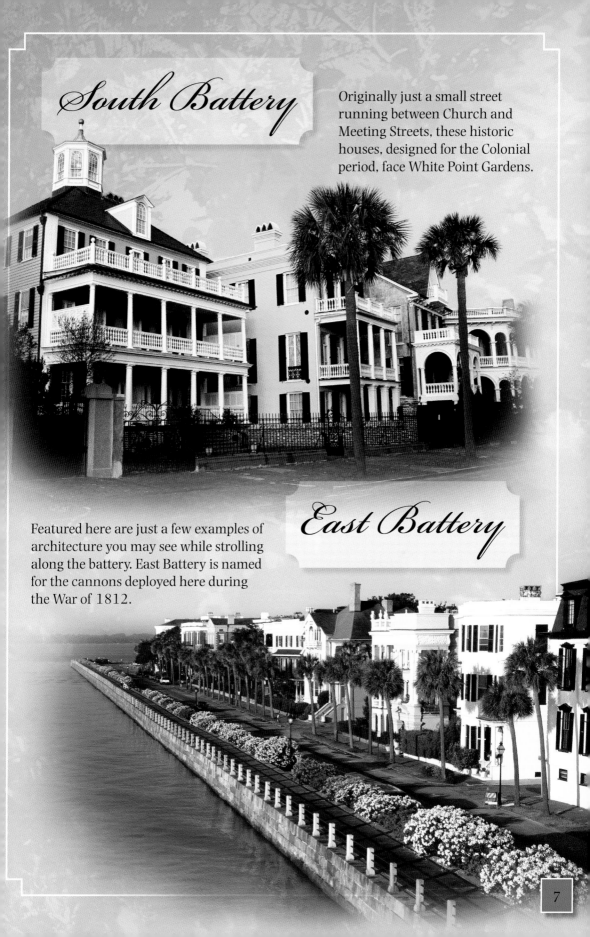

South Battery

Originally just a small street running between Church and Meeting Streets, these historic houses, designed for the Colonial period, face White Point Gardens.

East Battery

Featured here are just a few examples of architecture you may see while strolling along the battery. East Battery is named for the cannons deployed here during the War of 1812.

Rainbow Row

Rainbow Row is a quaint row of houses along East Bay Street which originally housed the owner's residence above their street level business. Typical of the English type of architecture, these double houses are of 18th century aspect. The houses, by owner's choice, are painted in a rainbow of colors.

Citadel Square Baptist Church

Citadel Square Baptist Church was founded on May 29, 1854, by fourteen people. Still in use today, the original house of worship was dedicated on November 23, 1856. It is amazing that a congregation of 217, 119 of whom were slaves, had a vision to build a sanctuary which seats 1,000. Because of its lovely Byzantine design and wonderful acoustics, Citadel Square was known as the finest Baptist house of worship in the South. The sanctuary was used as a Confederate hospital during the Civil War.

The French Huguenot Church, a National Historic Landmark, is the third church to be constructed on the site. The first was built in 1687 and the third and last structure was completed in 1845. It was the first Gothic Revival building constructed in Charleston. Today's congregation is the only French Calvinist congregation in the United States.

French Huguenot Church

St. Michael's Church

The oldest church edifice in the city of Charleston, the cornerstone of St. Michael's Episcopal Church was laid in 1752, and in 1761, the church was opened for services. This type of architecture is according to the tradition of Sir Christopher Wren. The clock and bells were imported from England in 1764.

Founded in 1681, the Circular Church, located at 150 Meeting Street, is one of the oldest continuously worshipping congregations in the South and has Charleston's oldest burial grounds with monuments dating from 1696. Its fourth and current structure is located on the exact site of the first "Meeting House" for which Meeting Street was named.

Circular Church

St. Philip's Episcopal Church

For over three hundred years, St. Philip's, the Mother Church of Episcopal Diocese in South Carolina, has been a vital and cohesive force in the Low Country. The present building dates from 1835. The 200-foot steeple, designed by Edward B. White, served for many years as an aid to navigation in guiding ships entering the harbor. The church yard is the resting place for John C. Calhoun, Vice President of the United States, and Edward Rutledge, signer of the Declaration of Independence.

Middleton Place

Thousands of spring-blooming azaleas reflect in the water of the Rice Mill Pond at Middleton Place. A National Historic Landmark, Middleton Place encompasses America's oldest landscaped gardens, the House Museum and working Plantation Stableyards, where craftsmen demonstrate the tasks vital to plantation life.

Magnolia Plantation
and its Gardens

Magnolia Gardens, once a rice plantation, is now one of
the world's leading gardens, having included the beauty
of the natural landscape in its informal design.

Boone Hall Plantation

This beautiful house is located on a grant of land from the Lords Proprietors that was given to Major John Boone in 1681. Its famous Avenue of Oaks and nine original slave houses add to the visitor's enjoyment and the historic interest of this Pre-Revolutionary Plantation.

Drayton Hall

A National Trust Historic Site, Drayton Hall is considered one of the finest examples of colonial architecture in America. It is the only plantation house remaining on the Ashley River that survived the Civil War intact. The house features exceptionally rich hand-crafted detail and is preserved in almost original condition after over 250 years.

Angel Oak

This gigantic live oak tree is named for the original owners and is estimated to be more than 1,400 years old. It is thought to be the oldest living thing east of the Mississippi River.

Summerville

Located just 20 minutes from Charleston is Summerville. This beautiful gazebo, surrounded by flowers and walkways, is enjoyed throughout the year by residents as well as visitors.

South Carolina Aquarium

The South Carolina Aquarium, Charleston's most visited attraction, features thousands of aquatic animals from river otters and sharks to loggerhead turtles and colorful reef fishes in more than 60 exhibits, all representing the rich diversity of South Carolina from the mountains to the sea.

SOUTH CAROLINA AQUARIUM

Patriots Point
Naval and Maritime Museum

Located on Charleston Harbor, S.C., Patriots Point Naval & Maritime Museum is among the world's largest of its kind. Aircraft carrier *USS Yorktown* (CV-10), World War II's famous "Fighting Lady," is the flag ship of the Patriots Point Fleet. She was commissioned April 15, 1943, and fought in many historic battles. Visitors may also tour the heroic destroyer *Laffey*, WWII submarine *Clamagore*, Coast Guard cutter *Ingham*, and a Vietnam-era Naval Support Base.

White Point Gardens

Charleston's White Point Gardens has protected historic homes from the ocean for over 200 years. The Battery is host to thousands of tourists as well as locals each year. Fort Sumter and Patriots Point can be seen from here along with pleasure boats, waterfowl and historic homes.

Colonial Lake

The lake and its park were established in 1768 by an Act of the Commons House of Assembly. The lake is a favorite place for locals to stroll and jog.

Hampton Park

Adjoining the campus of The Citadel is a lovely city park. This early spring scene is typical, with the thousands of azaleas and dogwood trees that make Charleston so attractive in the spring.

Waterfront Park

On the banks of the Cooper River, Waterfront Park is a 12-acre park located on the east side of the peninsula city. The pineapple, a symbol of hospitality in the Low Country, is beautifully depicted in a fountain which is the central feature of the park.

Shem Creek

Well known for its shrimping fleet and great seafood restaurants, Shem Creek offers a spectacular view of the sunset.

Arthur J. Ravenel, Jr. Bridge

Opened in 2005, one year ahead of schedule and stretching 1,546 feet between the two towers of the Cooper River, the Arthur J. Ravenel, Jr. Bridge is North America's longest cable stay span. Replacing both the John P. Grace Bridge (1929) and the Silas N. Pearman Bridge (1966), the new bridge has 8 lanes of traffic and a 12 foot shared pedestrian and bicycle lane which overlooks the Charleston Harbor.

Fort Sumter National Monument

Fort Sumter was the scene of the opening battle of the Civil War on April 12,1861. After a 36 hour siege, the Union garrison, commanded by Major Robert Anderson, surrendered Fort Sumter and evacuated the following day. The fort was then occupied by the Confederates and remained in their hands until shortly before the end of the war.

Fort Moultrie
(1870-1898)

Following the Civil War, Fort Moultrie was modernized by the United States Army using the latest technology of the period. Earth covered magazines and huge muzzle loading artillery were placed inside the fort. These 15-inch guns are capable of firing a projectile weighing 434 pounds, 4.5 miles.

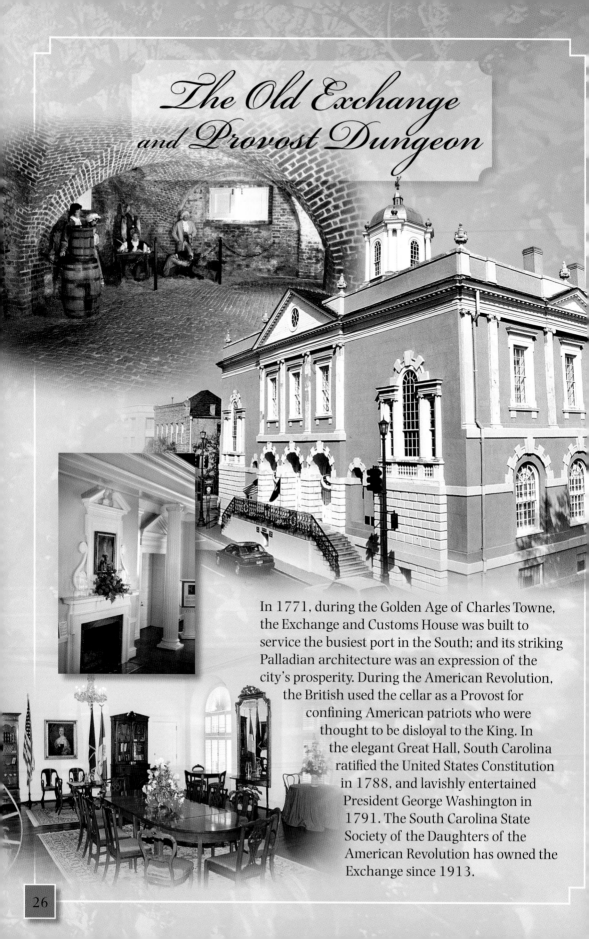

The Old Exchange
and Provost Dungeon

In 1771, during the Golden Age of Charles Towne, the Exchange and Customs House was built to service the busiest port in the South; and its striking Palladian architecture was an expression of the city's prosperity. During the American Revolution, the British used the cellar as a Provost for confining American patriots who were thought to be disloyal to the King. In the elegant Great Hall, South Carolina ratified the United States Constitution in 1788, and lavishly entertained President George Washington in 1791. The South Carolina State Society of the Daughters of the American Revolution has owned the Exchange since 1913.

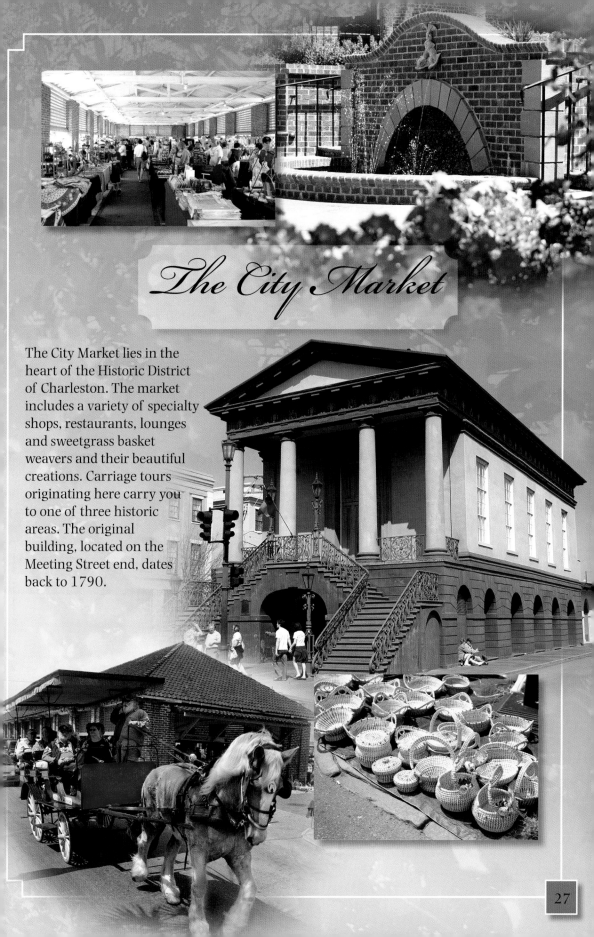

The City Market

The City Market lies in the heart of the Historic District of Charleston. The market includes a variety of specialty shops, restaurants, lounges and sweetgrass basket weavers and their beautiful creations. Carriage tours originating here carry you to one of three historic areas. The original building, located on the Meeting Street end, dates back to 1790.

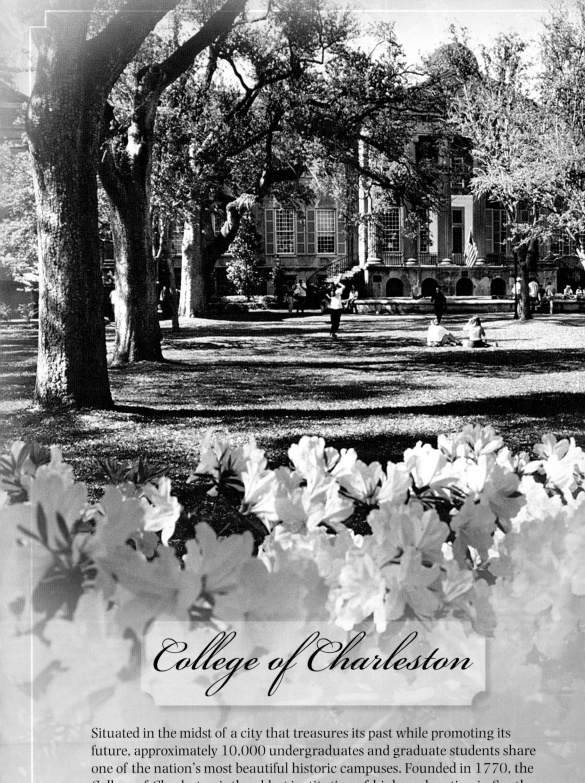

College of Charleston

Situated in the midst of a city that treasures its past while promoting its future, approximately 10,000 undergraduates and graduate students share one of the nation's most beautiful historic campuses. Founded in 1770, the College of Charleston is the oldest institution of higher education in South Carolina and the 13th oldest in America.

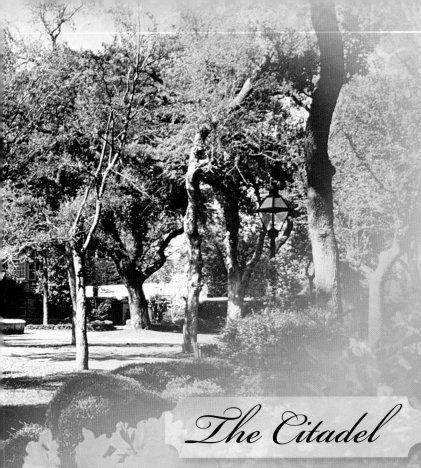

The Citadel

Founded in 1842, The Citadel, the Military College of South Carolina, is a comprehensive liberal arts college which includes a nationally recognized engineering program. The Citadel takes pride in educating the "Whole Person" - mind, body, and spirit; they achieve this goal through a rigorous fourth class system which is both challenging and rewarding. Here, Cadets stand at attention in formation while preparing for inspection prior to their weekly parade.

Folly Beach

The Pier, located 15 minutes from downtown Charleston, extends 1,045 feet into the Atlantic Ocean. Features include year round fishing, a restaurant and snack bar, a gift, bait and tackle shop, parking and restrooms. A unique diamond-shaped double decked platform at the end of the pier offers great views.

Sullivan's Island Lighthouse

Sailing, surfing, fishing and windsurfing are just a few of the activities along the coast of Sullivan's Island. Another famous barrier island, Sullivan's Island, attracts tourists to Fort Moultrie and its miles of beautiful beaches.

Morris Island Lighthouse

Morris Island Lighthouse, the original Charleston Light, is the sixth oldest station in the United States. With the original lighthouse of 1767 destroyed by the Confederate Army in 1861 to take a reference away from Union ships, the Morris Island Lighthouse was rebuilt in 1872. Standing 161 feet tall, when lighted could be seen 19 miles out to sea.